UNTITLED

STORIES OF CATHARSIS

AMALESH HONNEKERI

ISBN 979-888569881-8

To,

Everyone that had a part to play in this book.

Thank you.

Contents

Contents

Prologue

BEFORE YOU BEGIN READING THE POEMS –

Here's a guide to navigating this book:

We live in a world that is dynamic and fast-paced. The past decade has seen us witness change after change, some good and some.. not very desirable. We've been through a pandemic of mammoth proportions and witnessed the world evolve over the past few years.

'Untitled' is a collection of very unique poems. It represents a journey, one that is brimming with emotion, one that represents what a lot of us might be feeling, but are unable to express.

While the ending remains the most impactful part of this book, it is imperative to go through each poem in the order that is given, so as to truly experience this rollercoaster of thoughts.

Writing this book was a very cathartic experience for me. While I started working on this collection of poems a few years ago, having them published was never an idea that was on my mind. These poems are intimate, and based on my experiences, interactions with others and observations about the world around me.

I do hope that those who read this book are able to identify with what has been written, and use it as a tool for understanding their own feelings, and working on strengthening themselves from within. As you proceed with this book, you will notice an evolution of thought, and an acceptance of situations as they are. While there is no way to change an external locus of control, our internal response is what we can work on. And that is something I'd like all readers to keep in mind as they read this.

We cannot change the world around us, but we can take charge of how we interact with others. We can choose to be kind, for it is with acts of kindness that we can create a powerful ripple effect.

This book wouldn't have been possible without the constant encouragement I received from a multitude of well wishers. I'd like to thank my parents, sister, grandmother and aunt for their love and support.

Thanks are also due to all my friends, you know who you are. Thank you. And special thanks to my friend, Riya Vakil, who designed the cover of this book.

I'd also like to extend my gratitude to my teachers at the Cathedral & John Connon School and K.J. Somaiya Medical College, who have always had my best interests at heart and encouraged me to put my best foot forward in everything I do.

And lastly, thank you, dear reader, for investing your time in this book. I hope that you find within these pages a zone of comfort, a feeling of belonging, and a boost to your morale. Remember, as clichéd as it sounds - no matter how hard situations may be, "this too shall pass".

1. #1

Dark were the days that passed me by,
Cold was the wind every night.
Despair engulfed me like an oversized cloak,
Until from the nightmare, I awoke -

To a fragrance I had never smelled before,
To sunlight filtering through an open door.
To a song sung by birds in synchrony,
You pulled me from a place of misery.

But now in your absence, the night stretches on,
In the wake of your departure, I am forlorn.
Waiting for you to pull me out of this plight,
Waiting, as I tide through this stormy night.

2. #2

Did we really see this coming?
We were blinded by the brilliance of the sun,
As we dipped our feet in pool water;
Sipping on cocktails, prolonging happy hour.
Life was so blissful back then.

Did we really see this coming?
All we could hear was the echo of our laughter,
As each day passed by with carefree ease;
Planning vacations, the glitz and the glamour.
There were Subway runs that we can never forget.

Did we really see this coming?
The conversations that never had an ending,
Stories were shared from dawn to dusk;
Extending beyond the limits set by others.
Those conversations are but memories now.

You saw this coming, didn't you?
As step by step, you gradually backed out,

The sound of your footsteps diminishing;
While you reached the horizon, before disappearing.
You saw this coming, but I did not.

3. #3

Weathered,
Time and again.
Rained on, snowed on, stormed on
It stands resolute, in position.
However, as decades turn into centuries
And Time, that foe-like friend
Takes its toll,
Cracks appear.
The rock –
In all its resplendent brown and red glory
Slowly begins to crumble.
Unnoticed:
Unnoticed by the fowl
That journey by,
Unnoticed by the school boys
That strut by,
Unnoticed by the animas
That gather to predate;
This symbol of strength,
This once firm pillar of support,
Turns at last
From stone to sod.

4. #4

On and on
The horizon stretches,
The vast desert limitless.
The lone wanderer travels –
Travels in the direction of light.
Lips parched, eyes gleaming,
Back cold with sweat,
He walks on –
Confident, resolute, determined.
But, alas!
The desert is limitless.
As each dune crest
Falls to form a trough,
And the sand flies
Like a swarm of bees;
Angry and full of vengeance,
The lone wanderer takes cover.
As day turns to night
And the cold sets in,
As each oasis
Turns out to be but a mirage,
As each drop of sweat
Dehydrates him;

He finally realizes:
The way is but lost.

5. #5

The ticking of the clock intensifies.
Each moment passes –
The rolling of years
Akin to the blinking of an eyelid.
The fruits of labour turn sour
As the world crumbles to dust.
Panic echoes –
Like the wailing of mourners
Crying for that which is forever lost.
As the waves roll away,
Leaving behind dry sand;
As moisture-laden winds recede,
Leaving behind torrid ether;
As footprints fade away,
And Dawn turns to Dusk;
Time moves on, still oafish and surly,
And the clock remains resolute
In its unyielding sortie.

6. #6

Brimming up
Like the monsoon floods,
Slowly, steadily
Then all at once
Overflowing –
Spilling down miles of agony,
Watering the seeds of despair,
Plunging down loneliness
And landing in a heap –
Alone, broken, bare.
Tears – salty and cold,
Composed of molecules of spite, anger and fear
That coalesce.
One by one
They splash onto the floor,
Forming an ocean of woe.
As each drop adds to the sinkhole,
It grows –
Grows till it attains limitless depth,
Grows till it makes its creator
Appear diminutive,
Grows until it finally
Consumes him.

7. #7

The gloom sets in
Seemingly infinite.
All avenues exhausted,
The darkness builds up
Forming an abyss of despair.
The night is quiet
And black as coal,
The atmosphere eerily calm,
Foreshadowing impending doom.
Helplessness sets in –
A precursor to the raging storm.
As Anxiety, that merciless monster
Takes to the streets,
Destroying all in his wake;
I run looking for a sanctuary.
But, fuelling my dread,
I realize, perhaps too late;
The night is quiet
And black as coal,
And I,
Must keep running.

8. #8

The million-dollar smile
That lit up every room.
The charming indulgent laugh
That warmed every heart.
Charisma reverberating
With every step he took.
Happiness – Pure, unmarred, unblemished?
In reality, that was not so.
Behind every chirpy hello
He hid a tearful goodbye.
Behind every one-armed hug
He hid a bitter blow.
Behind all those walls of pretense
Lurked a crane waiting to tear them down.
All alone, in his soul
Behind the veil of glamour,
Behind curtains that masked
The fragility of his heart
He was lonesome,
Afraid of the eternal dark.
And so he was, in his resplendent glory –
All for the world,
But none for himself.

9. #9

Indecisiveness sets in –
Draining like a plug
All remnants of life within.
Into the endless hole tumble
Sanity, serenity;
In sinks Jove's own messenger,
Depleting the contents of every soul.
As the roaring of waves
Crescend to a cacophony –
All senses lost, every limb paralysed,
The abyss finally sets in,
Consuming:
Consuming all in close proximity,
Consuming massless spirits
By the masses.
The contents of Pandora's box reign supreme
And the battle is lost by Hope.

10. #10

The waves roll on,
Washing the rocks;
Foaming as they reach the shores,
Rinsing with them
The burdens of the world.
Litter decorates them,
Children marvel at them,
While lovers caress before them.

The dark night sky –
Black as coal
Stretches endlessly, its borders undefined.
The stars adorn it,
Forming an intricate pattern,
Each representing the Universe's design.

Under the sky,
And in front of the waves
He sits lonesome and forlorn.
Drowning under the lilt of the music
His veins imbued with rum.

Sitting there on the shore
In the groundless hankering that
The waves will atomize his pain,
And the sky, manducate his sorrow.

11. #11

Beneath the façade of jovial disposition,
An isolated heart beats.

Mirth, the domino of despair,
All the while, desolation underlies the carapace.

Among the coterie of many,
The sensation of alienation amplifies.

Cold is the heart that lacks a hearth,
Hyperborean is the heart sans propellant.

The donning of a smile, akin to the arraying of faux fur,
While discountenance silently plays the role of the inner.

As lustrous is the light that shines ostensibly,
So is the penumbra cast by the pitch prodigiously.

12. #12

The onset of Autumn brings with it
Fallen branches and scattered leaves.
It watches over as the forest floor fills up,
As it welcomes dryness, it slowly grieves.

The onset of night brings with it
A chill in the air, an ominous breeze.
As weary travellers retreat towards shelter,
A nightly poison shrouds the trees.

The senescence of something beautiful
Is always accompanied by mourning,
Tears well up as a farewell is bidden,
With a silent acceptance that there will be no returning.

13. #13

The ghost of your smile
Haunts the realms of my imagination.
Lingering, almost a reality, and
Then all at once – Fading
Fading
Into the depths of darkness,
Into draughty demise.
Blending
Into dreary monochrome.
With tears to wash away
The stains left by your blood;
Left with the memories of a riant era now gone,
I bid you farewell, O beloved one

14. #14

Built along the foundations of faith and trust,
Tethered down by nails resistant to rust.
The bricks were laid, adhered to cement,
Slowly and powerfully it rose –
The Unbreakable Monument.

Cyclones charged, tornadoes were a tradition,
Storms bore testament to the Monument's indestruction.
Berated time and again by hostilities galore,
Resolute stood the Monument –
Infrangibility radiating from its core.

However as disingenuous Time did traverse,
Bringing with it a levy of assaults onerous.
The nails wore out, the foundation weakened,
As under one ultimate blitz –
Beam by unbreakable beam, it turned succumbent.

In the aftermath as the tides recede,
Leaving behind detritus of pillars newly cleaved.

The dust settles, not romanticized by a background score,
The Unbreakable Monument now broken –
Its immortal foundation exists no more.

15. #15

At night, in the pitch of quiet,
Reflective is my state of mind.
Thoughts roll over like waves in a high tide,
Taking me back to a time sublime.
As my eyes caress the constellations above,
Drinking in their brilliant light,
The harrowed corridors of my mind
Are lit up by memories of occasions bygone.
The ticking of the clock, echoing in the silence
Serves as a memoir of more blithe junctures.
Engulfed in a duvet of reminiscence I lie,
As my heart pounds with an incessant yearning.
Suddenly, the plug is pulled,
Setting the drain into motion.
One by one, each fragment of nostalgia
Circulates in a whirlwind, before it vanishes.
Back to the present, my mind is alerted,
As sleep the analgesic finally takes control,
Into the realms of stupor I disappear,
With the anticipation of reanimating
To bear witness to a propitious hereafter.

16. #16

Underway,
Carrying a carousel of baggage,
Some extremely light – akin to a feather,
The most, however,
Heavy.
Pace quickening, hearts racing,
Hoping to momentarily forget –
Forget the floods that drowned humanity,
Forget the fires that consumed home and hearth,
Forget the desolation that was left behind.
The treacherous hand of Time,
Awhile hastening, awhile receding –
Considerate to the pleas of none.
The calm before the storm?
Perhaps disquiet is perpetually destined for some.
The wait must be borne
As the clock resumes its ticking,
The earth continues to spin on its axis,
Dispassionate as always.

17. #17

The nightly silence is pierced –
The creaking of crickets play culprit.
Tumultuous waves crash against the rocks,
While the wind strips the trees off their leaves.

18. #18

A bond built on the pillars of laughter and tears,
One meant to withstand the trial of years.
A friendship indescribable to anyone who asked,
Rested on a foundation that was expected to last.

Struggle after struggle made the earth 'neath tremble,
As crack and crevice ruptured, turning all to rubble.
Each blow leaving terrible desolation in its wake,
The fall from grace too subterranean to recalibrate.

Amidst the dust and debris, a lone voice cries for aid,
Oblivious to the bystander, in ruins it does wade.
The agony magnifying with every passing juncture,
As the last vestige of esteem ultimately does rupture.

19. #19

Trails of dust glistening, bedazzling
Frail and dirty, yet uniquely enticing.
In a rhythmic pace, forward they sojourn
No ounce of hesitation as they tread on.

20. #20

The cry like Pan in battle-
Horrific, yet inaudible to the mortal ear.
Shredding to pieces every fibre of his being,
Carrying with it the entirety of his soul.
An urgent call for nothing but assistance –
Somehow failing to ignite a signal,
Bouncing off the top of every head,
As unnoticed as an individual fowl in a flock.
The loops and bends increase in number,
As the road ahead gets but murkier,
Lit up only by remnants of fires now burnt out,
He trudges ahead, all the while shredded in doubt.

21. #21

Raging, raging into the dawn,
With hopes on a pedestal none could dethrone.
Spirit ignited, spreading like a forest fire,
New quests to conquer, heart filled with desire.

Spinning on its axis, as the year forged on,
At half revolution, half the battles were won.
New prospects of victory, battles fought triumphantly,
In the face of success, was a sum paid internally?

As Judas played visitor, baring a scabbard,
Not even his kiss could extenuate the blow to the knackered.
In one sweeping moment, friend turned foe,
Betrayal and Deception, each leaving a throe.

As one revolution finally comes to a close,
With gratitude and grace, we bid the past adios.
For lessons were learned, victories unmarred by loss,
With new zest and outlook, we nurture a legacy to emboss.

22. #22

Into the winter's night,
My thoughts drift unto the stars.
Floating at a snail's pace,
Onwards and upwards, towards ceaseless horizons.

Sticks and stones and weapons of every kind,
Reverberate in battle, yet heard by none.
As sanguine and lachrymose thoughts wage war,
Each hoping to conquer my mind's terrain.

The stillness of the night sky stirs up a storm,
The chill in the air, sharp as a tack.
As I gaze at the limitless expanse of the night sky,
I take in my relative diminution;
And I stand there, looking on –
A mere speck against the backdrop of eventide.

23. #23

Somewhere along the edge of the forest,
A spark ignites, spreading slowly.
As twig by twig, it begins to rage,
Proliferating from bush to tree, it augments.
Animals flee before the blazing colossus,
As the inferno incites a sense of peril.
Onwards it forges, pulverizing and destroying,
Blustering, as it rises to a treble.

24. #24

You are -

A sip of my favourite white wine:
Sweet and intoxicating,
Pure nectar to my soul.

Sunlight in a cloudless sky:
Filling the atmosphere with your warmth,
Your brilliance unparalleled,
Your radiant aura limitless.

A box of melted chocolates:
Filling all my senses with your essence,
As I drink in your delightful aroma.

Hope in my Pandora's box:
Anchoring me to a realm of positivity,
Ensuring that with you around, I am not lost.

25. #25

The thing about pain is
It comes in unannounced,
Bringing with it the gift of anguish.
Spreading out like the roots of an acacia,
Far and wide, soaking up sanity
As though it were water in a drought -
Taking all of it and sparing none.
It sits back as though it were Hades
Overseeing the lost souls of Tartarus -
Inflicting crippling torture on those it deems damned.
For, there is no escape from this abyss,
Resilience is the only fuel helping the pained power through.
But when that fuel eventually depletes,
What must one hold onto, to escape eternal doom?

26. #26

Sinking, falling into emptiness,
A cold heart silently grieves.
As turmoil sets in steadily,
Consumed by a premonition of unease.

The hollowness augments itself abruptly,
While the pit of doom seems infinitely deep.
Slowly, the shroud envelops the ensemble,
As the cliff of melancholy appears increasingly steep.

27. #27

The china vase stood resplendent -
The centrepiece amongst other finery.
Majestic and unique, made fastidiously,
It was one that could not be duplicated.

One gust of wind brought an end to it all -
As it fell to the floor, tumbling:
Dragging down with it years of toil and ardor,
None could make the save, as it hit the earth.

The noise reverberated, filling the air,
Like thunder, hailing a storm.
As a crack spread across its elegant surface,
Spreading out, stopping only at its core.

The china vase still stands in position,
The crack filled in by epoxy resins.
There now lies an alien beauty in its brokenness,
But the heart yearns for its former effulgence.

28. #28

Does it ever occur to you -
That behind that deceptive smile,
A shattered heart quietly beats?

When you hear the sound of roaring laughter,
Do your ears also tune in the muffled sobs?

Underneath all those layers of fine garment,
Can you sense the pain of ragged scars?

When you sip on sugary sweet dessert wine,
Do your taste buds catch the salt from tears?

Underneath the veil of impostrous beauty,
Are you aware that there lies a damaged soul?

29. #29

The world is -

A cauldron, bubbling with diversity:
A pinch of culture, A dash of tradition,
Altogether with vast geography.

A battleship:
Armour up high, defences ready,
Forging ahead in all its might,
As it traverses through stormy seas.

A rollercoaster ride:
Making stomachs churn,
In ways that are magical,
And sometimes dreadful.

A crowded theatre:
Full of chatter, completely abuzz,
Until the lights go out,

Ushering in a dark silence.

A patient in a hospital:
In need of care and consideration,
Waiting on better days ahead,
Waiting to feel the warmth of compassion,
Waiting to see sunlight fill up tomorrow,
Waiting, with no choice but to wait.

30. #30

We met in a strange place,
You broke me at my peak,
Left me shattered and aching
When I least expected it –
We met when I was unprepared to be met.

And here you are –
My constant companion,
Quarantined with me
In a quarantine that's lasted months.

You are the pit deepening in my stomach,
The palpitations making me tremble,
The background noise that never dies down,
The monster under my bed that never lets me sleep.

You've taken me down a dark alley,
Troubled me to no end.
You've brought me down on all fours,
But my heart and soul, I need to mend –

For I refuse to live a life of brokenness,
I need the broken pieces to coalesce.
You need to leave my life for good,
I need back my peace and solace.

For, I am a force to be reckoned with,
I've faced you before and won.
You bounced back stronger and attacked me,
But I have a powerful weapon – my Fortitude.

My Fortitude can move mountains,
Shatter ceilings and break down doors.
My Fortitude will unite me with my happiness,
And you'll go back into your hole.

When you're gone and my Fortitude has won,
I'll be living in sunlit meadows,
Drinking a bottle of my favorite dessert wine,
Rejoicing –
Knowing that in the end,
My happiness was worth the struggle.

31. #31

It's twelve o'clock on a moonless night,
Not a star to be spotted in the sky.
Still is the air that floats through and by,
While a loan candle lights up the night.

Somewhere in the woods, a fox searches for his prey,
While the candle burns, oblivious to it all.
The fox moves stealthily, no sound from his foot-fall,
As he pounces and devours his helpless prey.

The clock strikes four and the night is still dark,
Wax drips from the candle like blood.
As the candle wick burns out amidst a waxy flood,
Until it is extinguished, consumed by the dark.

32. #32

There's a light at the end of the tunnel,
It shines through a crevice, inviting me.
I stumble as it draws me nearer,
As I yearn to finally be free.

There's a light at the end of the tunnel,
Silence reverberates, echoing raucously.
As I reach out to bask in its luminescence,
All goes dim – did it consume me?

33. #33

Scattered on the pavement they lay,
Debris from the previous night's storm.
Roofs detached, bricks strewn all over,
Walls caving in, overpowered beyond their strength.

As the people inhabiting this dwelling
Came to survey the monstrous mess,
Their dewy eyed gaze taking in the sight
Of years of labour torn down and turned to dust.
Their minds were firmly resolute –
They would not bow down to this loss.
And thus started a new journey –
The journey of Rebuilding.

New bricks were lathered with cement,
As the people held onto each other for support.
For when Destruction had done its worst,
It was no match for their spirit:
A spirit that fought hard and long,
A spirit that overcame adversity,
A spirit that was blazing like an inferno,

But most of all –
A spirit that refused to cease.

34. #34

Why do your eyes look so sad?
They stare unyieldingly, devoid of their unusual cheer.

Your clothes seem to be hanging loosely,
As they flatter your form no more –
A form that once did them justice.

You're 24 but life seems to have taken with it
The jovial disposition of your youth.

You ask me but one question –
"When will I be happy again?"
A simple statement,
But with such complex implications.

And in that moment,
I find myself choking with emotion,
As I finally muster up the courage to say –
"It may feel like years,

But it's really only a few days.
Your heart will be healed,
All the pain shall drain away.
But to see that day,
You must fight –
Fight, for the inevitable end to this battle
Will be a victorious one for you."

We're surrounded in that moment
By sunlight streaming in through the window,
A stark contrast to the darkness lying in your heart,
It's urging you to let it in.

The atmosphere, though bright,
Seems cloudy with events and memories intense,
A cloudiness which has been hanging over you,
But it seems to be aware of its ending –
It knows it will be broken through –
Once the sunlight has been allowed inside.

What do you fear?
Is it the fear of professional failure?
Do you fear being alone in the dark?
Have your experiences led you to fear

The idea of ever opening up your heart to another?

Here I am, ready to fight the Demons –
Demons that have plagued my mind.
Here I am, having tasted defeat,
Prepared more than ever
To reclaim my happiness.

Here I am reaching out to you –
Promising you, with all my heart,
As I leave you with this thought:
"What has been lost will be regained twice over and more."

And now you leave me with
An album full of memories
A reminder –
Your happiness is worth fighting for.

I smile to myself,
Intoxicated by my thoughts.
As I pull my car out of your driveway –
And steer it straight home.

35. #35

For the longest while now,
I seem to be racing against time.
Racing, without intending to,
All the while bearing what seems to be
The weight of the entire world.

We go through the daily struggle and grind,
Working ceaselessly with no recognition.
Yet, we toil away as we are accustomed to,
For without us, how would life move on?

I seem to have grown in the recent past –
A growth that's almost detrimental.
I bear within my bulk, a pit unending –
So much depth, yet no real substance.

We tread the earth everyday,
Expected to stand stable and strong.
As we lumber about without complaint,
Trying our best to be unbreakable – do we not?

I am constantly visible to the world,
Too sharp, too fat; when are they ever content?
Constantly in motion, I power through the day,
For it is my motion that helps animate a drab world.

36. #36

I am going down a narrow lane,
A path that is shrouded by trees.
With sunlight filtering through the gaps,
Through darkness and in light,
The gravel and leaves crunch underneath my feet.

A path that is rarely travelled on,
I must go through the route perilous.
As I walk on, searching,
Hoping that the yield overthrows the jeopardy.
For is it not that one must swim through a storm,
To reach the island of paradise?

In sport we often get to see
Athletes taking the plunge as the crowd cheers on.
Yet, when I seem to bypass these lanes around me,
All I hear is but a scream.

This road is definitely a daunting one –
There is a reason it is left avoided.

For many have tried to venture forward over it,
But the destination always seems eons away.

The slight stream of light cascading in
Illuminates the ginger leaves now senescent,
That lie before me as I trudge on,
Their senescence but seemingly ominous.

Have philosophers not stressed on occasion
That the beauty lies not in the destination
But in the unraveling of the journey?
For all I can do is make merry –
Push through with a song on my tongue,
While my footsteps tap to my own tune.

Is it not the secret of life
To make one itch and prostrate before its kingdom?
As I walk, I realize I'm not alone –
Isn't that a pickup truck's horn somewhere in the distance?
Perhaps…

37. #37

Why are your eyes cast downwards,
Refusing to allow anyone a peek at them?
As you sit across me, clad in red and black,
Are these mere colours?
Do they represent a wider view?
Twenty-two and still growing up –
The age where all was made and destroyed.

You sit on the threshold of conflict,
Asking me if happy endings exist,
Wanting to know when dawn will break –
After all, it has always broken out before.

I tell you, as honestly as I can,
That your path will clear out,
The importance lies in walking along.
For you have felt defeated before,
And yet, here you are – aren't you?

The air is tense, silent as silent can be.

The light enters in abundance,
Casting itself across the hollows of your cheek,
Drying up your tears, drop by drop.
Your fears come to the fore –
Abandonment, anxiety, hurt;
Loss that is irreconcilable –
Are these fears not rational?

But here I am, sitting across you,
Urging you to give life another chance,
Urging you to explore as you move on,
For in exploring, you will find what you seek –
The challenge merely lies in moving along.

I take your leave, embracing you,
And as I go, I whisper into your ear –
"This statement is old and often used,
But in it lies a universal truth:
This, too, shall pass."

And now I stand outside,
Staring down at what you gave me –
A thermos flask, complete with a note:
"Hydrate," it says, "Don't forget."

Finally, I get into my car,
Ready to take off to a new destination.
Where am I headed?
To greener pastures.

38. #38

Patience is –
A long way from being home.
An examination, tougher than most.
An end-goal, remote yet desirable.
A virtue, one whose absence has cost me.

Uncertainty:
Am I good enough? Will I ever be?
How do I make my world revolve right?
A plague; making me stand on the edge,
As I look down on a canyon –
Is it really welcoming me?

Hope.
Sometimes my best friend, sometimes my nemesis.
When it shatters, all feels lost,
When it is present, is it really true?
"Hold onto hope," they say,
As my stubborn mind refuses to let go –
Sometimes, against better judgment.

Exhaustion,
Sometimes, at the end of a long day,
Inviting me to treat myself to relaxation.
Yet sometimes, my body does not feel it,
For it gets entangled within the fibres of my soul,
Screaming at me to settle down.

Self-love;
Our final and ultimate friend,
The driving force behind the feeling of mirth.
Yet, we tend to be so deficient in it –
For only in embracing it, can we truly be home.

Anxiety is:
Waiting on bad news, as the clock ticks frustratingly slowly.
Those palpitations that overpower your being,
The voice in your head that refuses to be silenced.

Friendship is –
A warm hug on a cold, stormy night,
Hot chocolate on the rainiest of days.
The foundation underlying love and trust,
The antidote to the most venomous of poisons.

Rest is
Putting your feet up on a leg rest,
Gulping down water after a long workout,
Peace and solace after a storm of overthinking,
Closing your eyes and letting time stop for a while.

Vitality is:
A necessity often mistaken as a luxury.
A birthright, one that's denied unfairly.
A retreat after going down a stony path.
A feeling I wish I would experience more often.

Peace is –
Sparkling windows after a much-needed wash.
A day at the spa, luxurious and indulgent.
A force that can end all worldly suffering.

The future is –
An entity that needs careful construction,
A lighthouse standing out during a night at sea,
Promises made that need to be delivered,
The final destination for an armament of prayers.

I am
A force to be reckoned with,
Capable of bringing about a change for the better.
As I walk this path, sometimes laden with thorns,
Sometimes carpeted by a bed of blue roses.
I stop by and say to myself –
I am
Always going to do my best.

9 798885 698818

Printed by Libri Plureos GmbH in Hamburg,
Germany